MY LIFE WITH MY GOD AND GODDESS

NANNI

INDIA • SINGAPORE • MALAYSIA

ISBN 979-8-89133-435-9

MY LIFE WITH MY GOD AND GODDESS

IN THE LOTUS FEET OF

MY GOD IN HUMAN FORM

DOULATRAM

(12.01.1924 – 06.03.2015)

MY GODDESS IN HUMAN FORM

KRISHNA

(05.02.1925- 11.09.2015)

PREFACE

Each book has a story to tell.

Every life has an experience to share.

We come in this world with our fists closed, but depart with our hands open, significant of the fact that we are born like a king, but die as paupers. As a famous Hindi saying goes: A closed fist is worth a million, an open one is worthless.

We do not take back anything with us. And this journey between our arrival and departure, is called LIFE. It should be our endeavour to make this journey beautiful with positive sentiments and emotions with our family and friends.

Let our journey be immortal and worth remembering.

ACKNOWLEDGEMENTS

This journey, called life, introduces you to many people, many noble souls.

On the crossroads of life, some remain as acquaintances, whereas there are many with whom you share a special bond.

I have met many such noble beings who have made a beautiful emotional bond with my parents.

My head bows down in gratitude to:

- My wife who has always taken care of my parents whole-heartedly and with devotion.

- My children who have been my pillars of strength and have been very close to my parents.

- My relatives who had a special bond with my parents and who made the lives of my parents happy.

A Parent's Love is Whole, No Matter How Many Times Divided

– Robert Brandt

PREAMBLE

The pages that follow are my experiences, moments in my life with my parents, and are absolutely true in their words, meanings and emotions to the fullest. I have tried to pen down the bond and the immense love and caring we had for each other. The journey of my life has been very sweet and memorable, thanks to my mother and father.

I am sure this book will have a universal connect with the hearts of the young and the matured, alike. We all have special moments in our lives, and who else know us better than our parents – our Makers.

I bow down in reverence and say thus:

Dukh sehna Maa Baap ki khatir, farz toh hai, ehsan nahin
Karz hai inka apne dil par, bhiksha ya koi daan nahin
Maat pita ke charan chooey jo, char dham tirath phal paavey
Jo aasis wo dil se de de, Bhagwan se bhi taali na jaave.

(source unknown)

I take this opportunity to thank everyone, who contributed to the happiness of my parents, special thanks to my wife and children.

Blessed are the children who have the blessings of their parents. Blessed are the children who have the good fortune of seeing their parents everyday.

Blessed are the children who can embrace their parents everyday, because that hug has so much warmth, purity and emotions, which is unparalleled, unmatchable and is beyond words that can explain the feelings of those moments.

Blessed are the children who know that their parents are their umbrellas to shield them from the heat, rains and storms of misfortune.

The loss of your near and dear ones is painful. And the loss of someone you adore, you look upon as GOD and GODDESS, is catastrophic.

The period - End of 2012.

Dad was diagnosed with Cancer. To contain the disease, some doctors suggested surgery. But due to his age and other physical considerations, our friends and relatives advised against it, even some medical opinions were not favourable, because post -surgery recovery was deemed doubtful. So, we put Dad on a dose of ayurvedic medicines which saw him through the next 2 years, though with some pain. Dad was a fighter. My Mom and Dad were ardent devotees of Sri Sathya Sai Baba, with full faith in HIM. And they had no malice for anyone, and with love for all.

Their love for me was without boundaries. I remember that, everytime I used to travel to Vadodara, and was delayed just a little, from the scheduled time, I would get a call from Dad enquiring my whereabouts. And frankly, I used to wait expectantly, to get his calls.

Whenever they were with us in Mumbai (Dad used to call Mumbai a concrete jungle), I would see the glow of happiness in their eyes. And their stay with us was very comforting. My very sight would make them happy, and younger by years. Their embrace, every time they hugged me, was so full and warm. Even in their declining years. No words needed to be spoken. Their eyes told me all.

A Note from the youngest brother of my father:

In early 1947 at the young age of 7, I heard my father (in those days father was called Baba and mother as Bhabhi) talking to his friends and others about India's struggle for Independence and how Gandhi was fighting the British through Satyagraha and the Non Violence Movement.

It was later on in life after having acquired more insight on the other aspects of India's freedom movement through history books amongst other sources did I realise that though Gandhi was indeed the driving force behind India winning Independence, there were other unsung heros who played a significant role right from the 1890's. It was then that the freedom struggle had got a kick start with many of these valiant citizens laying down their lives for the noble cause of freeing India from the British rule. This was not an easy task as the British was connived to divide India into different states and incited each state to fight its neighbouring state. It took the wise and calm heads of Gandhi, Nehru and other notable leaders of that time to unite the states (religious fractions) and be successful in their ultimate goal of achieving Independence.

INDEPENDENCE AND PARTITION

It was around the 1st week of August 1947, Bhabhi and me were staying with my brother Daulat. He was a supervisor in the Telephone Department and was friendly with a lot of influential persons, including the Station Master. Baba was posted as a Doctor in a nearby village. Other brothers and sisters were in our home town in where they were doing their schooling.

It was around that time that the division of Hindustan and Pakistan was announced. We also learnt then that India would be liberated from British rule and gain Independence on 15th August. Conflict between religious fractions had already begun and took a worrying and serious turn by mid September. While the local brethren residing in Province were friendly and maintained old relations forged over the years of living together, the brethren coming in from Punjab had started inciting their community.

Riots started all over and the Hindus residing there soon realised that they had no option but to make the difficult and unavoidable decision of leaving their homeland. My brother Daulat was advised by his local friends to leave as soon as possible, before the situation got further out of control. Consquenlty Daulat got his transfer orders to Lucknow and the Station Master assured him that he will arrange a small compartment in a train that will take us upto Barmer in Rajasthan, India.

Baba and Daulat went to bring back our family members. As young girls were being targeted my cousins and Dadi (my grandmother) came along with him. The bus journey from Hyderabad was quite harrowing. At Hyderabad and enroute they were made to open boxes and most of the clothes and jewellery were snatched and stolen from them. There was open looting in the train. Men were being beaten up, women sexually harassed. It took the best part of 2 days to cover a distance of 300 kms. Understandably as a consequence of this traumatic experience all of them were in a state of shock when they arrived.

It was around 10 years back while watching a film based on Partition that I realized how harrowing the bus journey my brother and sisters undertook while travelling must have been during which they were tormented and harrased. This realization was further reinforced during our train journey to Godra (India). Watching horrific scenes of families travelling on top of trains anxious, harrased, their faces bloodied. One cannot even begin to comprehend the agony and pain of leaving their homeland and starting life afresh with almost nothing, in most cases. Coming back to my memories of those times, as promised by the Station Master a small compartment in a train was arranged by him.

JOURNEY TO LUCKNOW

It was early October 1947, we were told to get into the bogie of the train the evening prior to its departure. Consquently all 10 of us reached the station around 4.00pm. The train we were supposed to travel in had just arrived from India. We were all seated in the station waiting room and at around 7.00pm we were taken to the bogie which was stationed in the yard. As there were no lights all the men stayed in the bogie overnight. Early next morning the rest of us made our way to the bogie.

As it had rained the previous night the money Baba had put inside his shoes for safety got wet, making a bad situation worse. The train with our bogie was brought to the platform in the afternoon next day. The commotion and the desperate rush of everyone wanting to escape resulted in the delayed departure of the train which left several hours (those hours felt like months for us wanting to leave) later at night. Daulat and my other brother were pacing up and down the platform to arrange for food for the journey. The prevailing uncertainty of when we would reach Barmer necessitated the arrangement of a lot of food.

As the train was filling up with hundreds of refugees we closed the doors and windows on the side facing the platform. There was a mad rush of people trying to get in but they were turned away on the grounds that the bogie was reserved for Government officials only. I remember the train finally leaving late at night. For those interminable 12-14 hours before the train left we felt like fugitives hiding inside. What I witnessed was exactly how it was depicted in the movies dealing with the Partition Era. Everyone was searched regularly. The police came to check too but Daulat managed to keep them at bay by showing a Pass he had managed to procure from the Police Superintendent earlier.

When I got up next morning I saw the bundles of notes which had got wet in Baba's shoes drying on the seats.

Whenever I see films or TV shows dealing with India/Pakistan partition or the Jews fleeing from Germany during the World War and how they depict trains packed to the rafters with people on the roof and compartments, it reminds me of the traumatic and frightening scenes of our journey. We were stopped at a station in close proximity to the border (Godra Road on the Indian side). The opposite side of the platform were trains going towards border presented a similar horrific sight. Those trains too were packed with people, their clothes bloodied, their visage haggard and scared. I was told only later that the scenes in our train were similar too.

Before Godra Road we had halted at Umarkut on the other side of the border at around 12.30pm. The train and its occupants were being thoroughly frisked by a group of men including Police. We escaped this checking as we were luckily in the reserved Bogie for Government officers. It was around 5-6.00pm when we left Umarkut. The journey of 60-70 kms to reach Godra Road (Indian side of the Border) took us the best part of 5-6 hours.

I had gone to sleep during the journey and woke up the next morning when I was told that we are now in India. The sense of relief on everybody's face was palpable. Daulat went out to arrange for some tea and food. From Godra we took a train to Lucknow via Jodhpur- Ratlam which took 2 full days.

Once we reached Lucknow, Daulat went to the office while the rest of us waited at the station. There was further bad news. Daulat was told that the residence alloted to him was not vacant. We finally managed to find a roof over heads in a dharamshala (guest house) where refugees were put up. We were alloted one big room whilst the toilet and bathing facilities were to be shared with the other inmates of the Guest house. The Guest house did not have provision for electricity and oil lamps were used at night as a substitute. Cooking was done in an open verandah on a brick choola using coal fire. These tough conditions were difficult to adjust to and it took us 2 months to come to terms with the same. Our story must have been similar to the other occupants of the Guest House as well, who to would have had to adjust to such a drastic change in their living conditions.

It was the Grace of the Almighty that Daulat had a job. It was his income that helped us survive and weather the storm. He along with my brothers and sisters had leant to converse in hindi.

3 months later Baba went back to to sell our house. My eldest brother helped them negotiate and close the deal for the house following which all 3 of them returned to India. We stayed in the Dharamshala for more than a year during which my brother got a Government job in Delhi. My cousin sisters joined their families. In 1949 a bungalow (2500 sqft of built up area + covered verandah and garden) was allotted to Daulat, wherein we finally settled.

One of the Greatest Titles in the World is Parent, and One of the Biggest Blessings in the World is to Have Parents to Call Mom and Dad

– Jim DeMint

MID-FEBRUARY 2015

Dad had not been keeping well, and I was with them at Vadodara. Cancer had spread in the body, and the medicines Dad was taking could contain the pain very temporarily. He used to complain of stinging pain at times, but I was helpless. All I could do was find a corner, and cry and cry.

4th March 2015

I remember this date very vividly. As I used to do, I embraced him tightly. He used to love my tight hug and would try to reciprocate. But that day, he just embraced me lightly and said: You are here, it's good. Don't go away. I kissed him and said I will stay here till you want and then we will go to Mumbai together. Little did I realize then, that, those were the last words I was hearing from Dad. He just ate a few spoonfuls. And he told me to take him to the washroom. Normally, whenever I used to take him to the washroom, he would hold my hands or shoulders and walk. That night, he just could not hold me. Somehow, I took him. When he was through, I took him by my hands and asked him to hold me, but he could not, in spite of many efforts.

I had no help. And Dad was not able to hold me at all. I hugged him and clasped him and succeeded to put him on the bed. Called out to him, he just opened his eyes, but said nothing. I called my brother-in-law, a Doctor, who advised hospitalization. Dad was hospitalized. Tests were done, were critical. And we had to put Dad on a ventilator. That was the time my heart sank, and I cried.... and kept on. I knew the end is near. All efforts to revive him, failed. We brought Dad home, on 6th March 2015 afternoon. Amid chanting of Bhajans, and in the presence of family and Sai devotees, he closed his eyes at 1 pm on 6th March 2015. And closed my doors to expect talking to him, seeing him, seeking him, embracing him, loving him and being loved.

Dad and Mom, you always used to say: We want to see Priyanka getting married. And Sagar settling down in a job. And we were fortunate, both your wishes were fulfilled in your lifetime. Now that you both are united with God, please bless the kids. Now whenever I look at the sky, I will seek your blessings (as also the blessings of Munna.... my younger brother whose demise has left a big void in my life).

Dad, you have influenced many lives. Condolences have been pouring in from people, I have not heard of, or met. Purity of your mind and soul, ever helping nature, smiling face is what everyone remembers. Sathya Sai devotees have a special respect and love for you. Thanks to them for their support.

With your passing away, Dad, life has come back full circle for me. Suddenly, I feel tremendous vacuum and void in my life, pangs of separation, feeling of loneliness and want, uncertainty. No one to embrace me when I am low. No one to look at me with wanton eyes, the sense of belonging and tremendous reassurance which you used to give me, The very thought of your bring alive, and with me and the confirmation of your blessings. Mostly unspoken.... But always felt and understood. Now no more.

Getting reprimanded if I did not call you, Dad? Who will scold me now? Who will show anger in his face, but love in his eyes? Whose hands will I hold and whom will I embrace to get comforted? Who will be my guiding light? Suddenly, all has vanished without a trace. And I know it will not come back. Nor will you, Dad. How easy it is for me or people to say that Dad is no more, or that he has lived his life, fully and happily. Or that one day we all have to go. But how difficult it is to come to terms with the fact that a person who was your friend, father and GOD –like, is not there with you anymore.

Is there life after death, I don't know, Is there life in death, I don't know. Is there an after-life, I don't know. But I do know for sure is, that I want you and Mom to be my parents in every life that God gives me. Dad, I don't know whether my life will be the same after your passing away. But, I am sure, you know the answer. Howsoever much I tried to hide my grief and my problems from you, I never succeeded. You always did read my mind, absolutely perfectly. That was the strength of our emotional bond,

Dad, I am sorry, I might not always, have been a good and true son. Though I tried to, I had my shortcomings. I wanted to be good, I tried my best to make your life comfortable. I don't know how much I could accomplish in my deeds. We wanted you and Mom to stay with us always.

Dad, you have always given me what I wanted in life. And you know that all I wanted was love. And that love and caring, you and Mom gave me in abundance, in fact, more than what I had wished for. I am fortunate to be your son. I am proud to be your son. I am privileged to be your son. I promise you that I and my family, will take care of Mom always.

Old memories are still very vividly clear in my mind. Like when you used to take us all (a family of 5) in a scooter, our homes at R K Puram, Defence Colony, Lajpat Nagar etc. hiding in pits in Delhi in war times, my booking 1AC tickets against your wishes, and you getting angry. Your telling me that you owned a 5HP BSA motorcycle, in Lucknow, way back in 1947. And that you were one of the few AIEE engineers of your time. These and other memories are permanently sketched in my mind.

Dad, as you have now made the Heaven, your abode, please look down from the sky occasionally and take care of us. Bless us. We all love you. We will continue to love you forever. It was a very little time in my life, when you needed my support to hold you. I wish the time could have extended. But GOD willed otherwise. HE knows better. God knew that such a beautiful and lovely soul should not suffer for long.

I meekly submit to HIS wish. I now pray to the Almighty to make me your {and Mom's} son, in every life that he gives me, in whatever form he gives me.

One secret I want to share with you today, Dad. Around the end of last month {Feb 2015}, I went to our Puja room and requested God that I should be with you, during the last moments of your journey of life. And HE ensured that I was with you. GOD listens. In those last moments, I saw you waving your hand, exactly like Sathya Sai Baba, and this told me all.

No one has seen GOD, but we believe in HIM. I have seen my GOD, and I believe in him, in YOU, Dad. You went away all of a sudden. Did not give me a chance to talk to you in those last moments. I don't know what thoughts you have taken with you. You were normally a quiet person. KEHNE KO BAHUT KUCH THA AGAR KEHNE KO AATE, APNI TOH YE AADAT HAI KI HUM KUCH NAHIN KEHTE. (extract of a Hindi song)

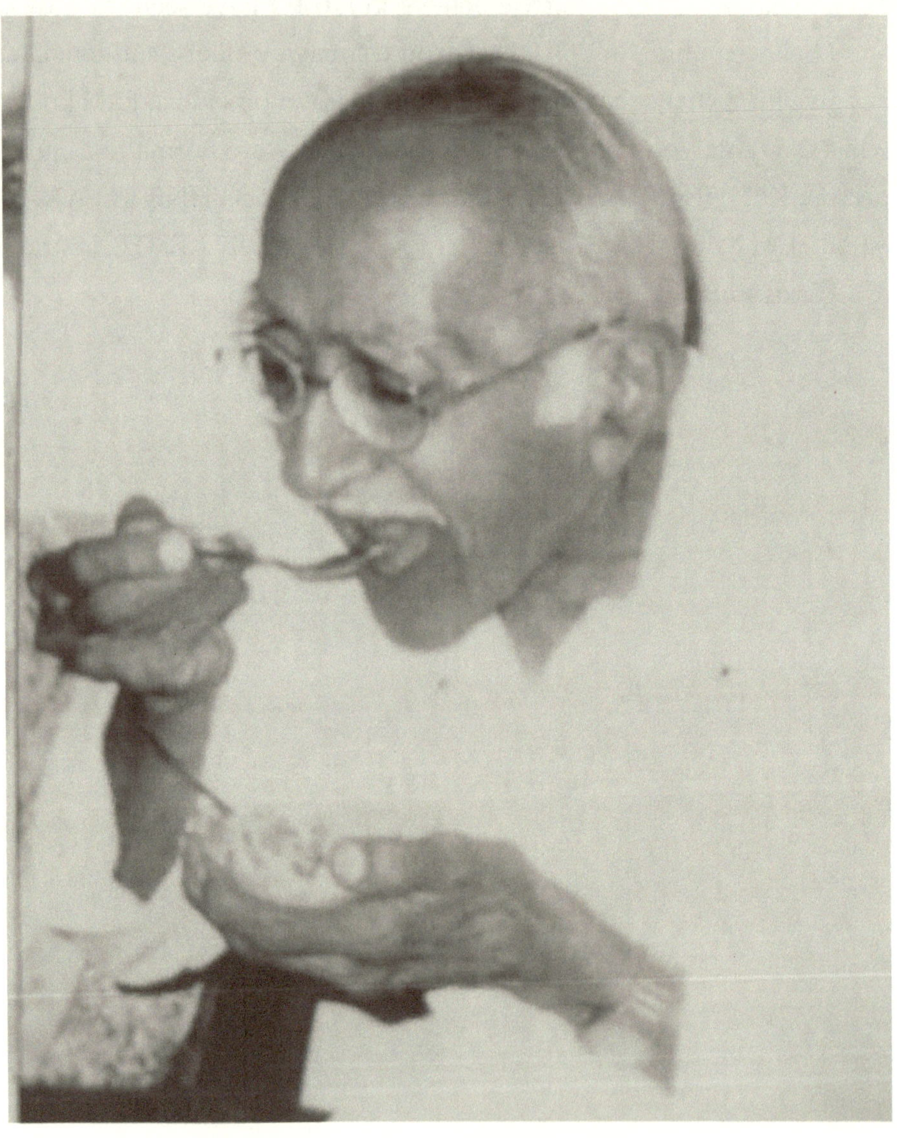

A self-made man that you were, you never asked for any help or assistance from anyone. Even till the end, you used to help people financially, even after your retirement. You lived your life happily, with contentment, were very jovial, easy-going and down-to-earth. People loved you for your openness. And their thoughts bear ample testimony to this fact. Even my MD, whom you met for a few moments only, on just a couple of occasions, had this to say:

"I regret not being with you, at the time of his demise. Your Dad was my good friend, and was young at heart and very practical. Losing people for whom you have love, affects me most. He was indeed a true gent. For you, I understand he is missing. The whole world seems empty. You must develop the rhythm of courage."

{Thanks, Mr. Shah, for your words}

An ardent devotee of Sathya Sai Baba for decades, Dad was hugely respected amongst the fraternity of followers of Baba. You were true to your name, Dad – DOULATRAM: DOULAT – a treasure to cherish, and RAM –God in human form. Such a lovely and unique combination.

After Dad's demise, because we had guests at home, I went to get some snacks from restaurants nearby. And guess what? The bill in each of the 2 restaurants was 108. Was it a coincidence? Or was if God's way of telling me that a pious and pure soul has reached him safely? Because Bhagwad Gita has 108 shlokas, the sacred mala has 108 beads, and Sai baba has 108 names.

Or was it Dad telling me: Son, I am resting in peace. May your soul rest in peace, my creator, my maker. Dad, as you are now united with God, continue giving us your blessings and unconditional love. I am sure all your aspirations have been fulfilled in your lifetime, so rest in peace, Dad. You believed in yourself. I BELIEVE IN YOU. Believe in the GOD who believes in you.

Dad, on 17th March, Priyanka saw you wearing a white safari, waving out your hands, and smiling. She wept bitterly. You said to her: Don't cry, I am fine.

Finally, Dad; Mom, and my family, join me in praying to GOD, the creator, to give everlasting peace to your soul. As you are now united with the MAKER, please pardon us mortals. We seek your pardon with folded hands, kneeling feet and a prayer on our lips.

Parent's Eyes Are the Reflection of Their Unconditional Love for a Child on This Earth

Source unknown

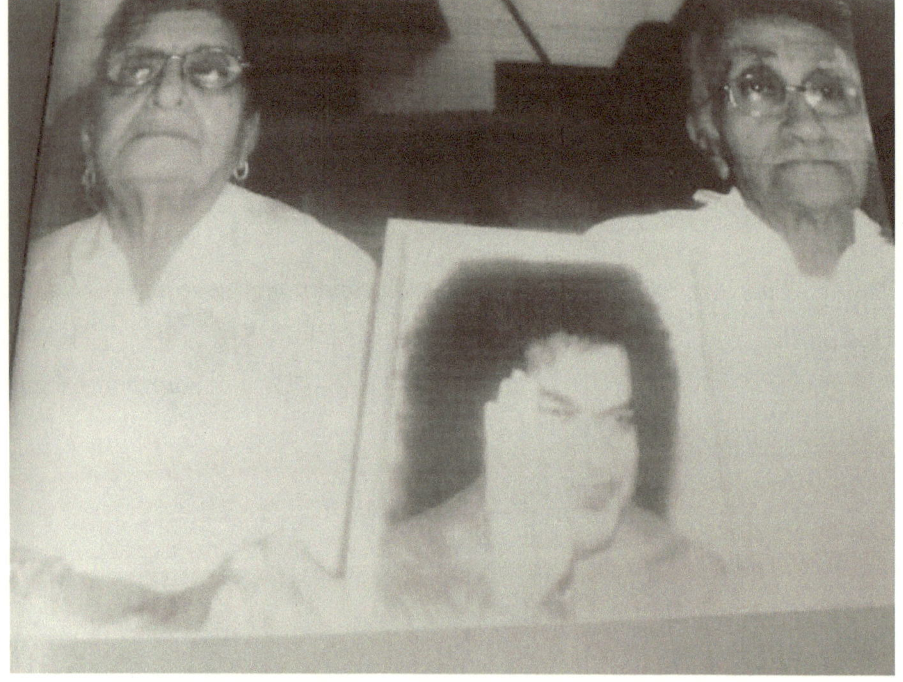

THE LAST JOURNEY

Today, 16 March 2015, dear Dad, me and Sagar started from home for immersion of your mortal remains at Chandod. I held the urn containing the ashes of your mortal remains. Imagine holding the remains of a soul, whom you have loved unconditionally, now confined to an urn. I held it close to my heart, as if I will not let you go. During which time, I wept… and wept… After I immersed your mortal remains in the Triveni, a flower from the garland which was in the boat, fell off.

Did you tell me that you are finally resting in peace? United with the MAKER?

LOVE YOU ALWAYS, MY DAD, MY GOD.

Condolences have been pouring in from relatives and friends, and show the extent of love they all had for you.

Someone says they have very fond memories. Some consider you as the most fun-loving person, party man who enjoyed everything in life. Yet another relative remembers the times you used to make tea for them, used to clean our home and took your illness in your stride. That you always used to wear a white shirt and white pants, and used to sing songs of Late Shri KL Sehgal and Late Shri CH Atma.

March 6th, 2015 was the dark day in my life when you left me all alone in this world. Of course, I had and have my family with me, who love me and care for me immensely. But the bond you had with me, the limitless love we shared, and which I could see in your eyes and in your smile, and which my heart could feel, was out of this world.

Over 4 months have elapsed since you departed, Dad; but there has not been a day when you have not been in my thoughts. I have shed tears quietly. Mostly there is a weep in my heart and a total void in my life. Your presence was so reassuring that I used to forget all the problems of my life.

Now, it is Mom who is my savior. Mom is with us and is being taken care of.

I am sure you are seeing it. She has been diagnosed with cancer, and is rather at discomfort. I try to keep her cheerful and happy. I know of the immense love you had for her, so please give her a happy life. I have seen you suffering in silence, Dad. You were strong.

I do not want Mom to suffer .... I am not that strong to see her in pain.

She has lost interest in life, after your departure. I try my best to keep her cheerful. She told me a couple of months back that she will not live for more than 6 months, after your demise. I again cried, and for the first time, got angry with her. And repented, almost immediately.

I have written so much of my experience of my life with you, but frankly, I have still not been able to express the real meaning of thoughts, of my love for you. Maybe, I will never be able to express. Because my love for you, Dad; was and is beyond words. It was felt. It was understood. It was sublime. It was ethereal. It was Godly. It was; Plain and true love. You have left such a powerful impact in my heart that I feel your presence everywhere.

Now whenever I go to Vadodara, and go to our Manjalpur home, I am lost. I have spent so many beautiful moments with you and Mom there. Be it helping Mom in the kitchen, or precious little heart to heart talk with you, of just resting in your and Mom's laps…. Enjoyed immensely. But now, empty rooms, only furniture and walls. No soul. But I can still imagine you sitting in the hall watching TV, making tea, sleeping on your side of the bed. But now I am not able to stay there for long. Too much emptiness there. Your memories keep coming back to me and make me sad.

I really don't know whether my life will, ever, be the same again. I think it never will be. There is no one waiting expectantly for me now, no one who loves me the way you did, no one to look forward to my calls and visits, no one to reprimand me and get angry if I did not call, no one to have happiness in his eyes on seeing me. I will miss every precious little moment, that you gave me in abundance. I am preserving all these moments in my heart and will cherish them throughout my life, Dad.

What a soul you were, Dad. Simplicity personified. Humanity personified. Humility personified. Brimming with emotions of love and caring. Why did you leave me all of a sudden? Why couldn't you stay for some more time? Why didn't you come to Mumbai towards the end of your journey? You deprived me of an opportunity and privilege to serve you in the end and you suffered.... Silently and within. I am sorry I could not lessen your suffering.

I vividly remember the times of my life I spent with you – our Bungalow at Kota, seeing snakes nearby sometimes, our stay at Delhi, going out to tours with you while you were in service. Those are priceless precious memories. But with your passing away, things have changed. I request your soul to normalize the events for me. It is very difficult for me to see anyone suffering – though it is quiet and not expressed. I am also human and have deep emotions, but I take a bold stance. Please bless my family. Please be the guiding light and spirit for us. We all are your children. Lead us .... Guide us, divine light.

From the time you have left us, events have led me to believe that you are near us, with us. Suddenly a crow started coming to us, from the kids' room to the hall as if wanting to come in. And waiting till it was fed. Maybe, it was you, coming to us, and wanting to see how Mom was. But suddenly the crow disappeared. Maybe, you now know that Mom is happy with us. I understand your concern for Mom, knowing well the immense and unconditional love you had for her. You were an embodiment of love. I share the same emotions of love for Mom.

Why were you so nice, Dad? Why did you have a heart of gold? Why were your emotions for me, so strong and immense? Now, I am unable to live without you. Life has lost its meaning.... Completely.

I might sound repetitive at times, during the course of my writing, but it is not in my control. I am just penning my thoughts as they come. And there is no stopping the flow of my thoughts. Because you did not have just faith in me, you had intellectual faith. Now, you have transformed into a soul, which has no beginning and no end, which is immortal. In fact, the home at Manjalpur where I had the best memories of my life with you and Mom, is very sacred to me, and I call it "The temple of love".

You know within your heart that I have never been interested in your property or money. All I wanted from you both was love. And that I got more than I wanted. Maybe, more than I deserved. And these worldly pleasures have no meaning for me. If only, now I could keep Mom happy, we are trying our best. And if I could give you peace in Heaven because of my deeds, I shall have fulfilled the meaning of my life. In fact, more than me, it is my wife who has taken care of you both, who has always been understanding, and who is now taking care of Mom, and I salute her for that. Also, my children, have loved you immensely and have been very supportive. We have grown up as a family, and living like one. Thank you, God, for such a lovely family.

Today, 26 July 2015. On my train journey from Mumbai to Jodhpur, I saw 2 sons taking care of their aged parents, making their beds, taking them for the call of nature, feeding them, putting blankets for them. It took me back in times, when we used to travel together.... I relived those moments, and my eyes could not stop shedding tears. I miss those moments now, and I know they will never come again in my life.

I know that I have not been very good as a person. Maybe, also as a son, as a husband, as a father. But I have not been all that bad, either. I have felt for everyone in my life, and I still do. Maybe because of my outbursts, I am misunderstood. But, I know my "within". My conscience is clear, and you are with me, Dad. Though I think I have tried to be a good son. I was lucky and privileged to have you as my father. I might not be that good, I know. But I sincerely hope I have been a good son to my parents. No one today, is a Sudama of mythological times, nor can we come close to their deeds and sacrifice. But we can make the lives of our loved ones comfortable, and I think I did my bit in that, Dad.

I remember the times when I was staying in a hostel for 3 years, and how you would have managed to send me money for my education, stay etc. Given the limited source of income you had, and also 3 children to be taken care of. But never a word or sign of discomfort from your end.

Life continues. Journey continues. Another journey today, 5 August 2015. And my memories travel back in time and I reminisce the moments I spent with you and Mom. These, and other countless moments are permanently etched in my memory. And seem as if they are happening right away, though I know these will never come again. And I shall wait for another life with you to relive these moments again. Sometimes; in fact quite often, I get a feeling of separation. And I feel like going towards "Vaanprastha". Towards seclusion, towards oneness with Almighty. Seek repentance for my sins committed during this life of mine. God willing, I shall do so, before I eventually meet my "MAKER". Maybe that way, I can again somehow come close to you, Dad.

Again, another journey. Revival of thoughts. One moment you were there with me and the next moment – Gone. Never was I mentally prepared. Though in those last 2 days, I could sense. But there was a total disconnect between my heart and mind. What my mind could sense, my heart would just not accept. Even today, I have yet to come to terms with your loss. I have yet not forgotten my younger brother Munna, who passed away in 1987. He is in my thoughts every moment. How can I forget you?

Priyanka writes: "Life doesn't always introduce you to the people you want to meet. Sometimes, life puts you in touch with the people you need to meet – to help you, to hurt you, to leave you, to love you, and to gradually strengthen you into the person you were meant to become." {Quote – Steve Maraboli}.

What a statement. So true with all of us. I was destined to meet you, to love you and be loved. I really couldn't help you much, hope I didn't hurt you, Dad and Mom. I have not left you. You have left me. And I am lost in wilderness.

Journey continues. A tea vendor passes by in my compartment. I ask for a cup of tea. And suddenly memories take me back to my travels with you, when you would insist the tea vendor to fill the cup completely and we would laugh and enjoy. And just now a strange thing happened. My train started moving after its scheduled halt at Sawaimadhopur station. And came to a screeching halt almost immediately. Guess what? I heard people saying that there was a small snake on the tracks under my compartment. Which was sent away safely. I remembered Kota. And was it a signal from your soul that you have heard my wishes.

And are guarding and guiding us. That no evil will come to us. That you are our savior.

Dad, in this life of mine, there was hardly anything that I could do for you and Mom. In fact, there was nothing I could do to make your life comfortable. And you were so large-hearted that my mere presence in front of you, made you and Mom happy. You never demanded anything, you never expected anything. Except love. And really, your happiness was reflected in the glow of your eyes. This is the reality of life. During my growing years and till today, I have seen you from a young handsome man to a mature person to an ageing being. I have seen your transformation from a glowing face to wrinkles. But one thing that did not change throughout this transformation was your love for me, for us. It was constant. It was Godly. You were divine, Dad. You are my darling.

Dad, it's over 5 months that you left us, but I still feel, you are with me. That you will call me. You will come to me. You will embrace me. You will kiss me. And I will just meekly submit to you.

That you will talk to me. That you will rebuke me for not calling you for so long. That you will wait for my coming home.

That I will wait for you to come to Mumbai with me. That I will wait for you to physically bless me.

Alas.... All this will not happen. And I know that my wait just got endlessly longer.... And impossible to end. But Dad, some final favours I request you:

Be with me.

Be with my family, always.

Be with us forever.... In whatever form you are.

And continue your blessings. We love you.

And I know, you love us... More.

And sometimes Dad, show us that you are around us, within us, with us.

Love you, Dad.

Love you my God.

REST IN PEACE.

6th September 2015

Today is exactly 6 months, Dad, since you left me. Mom is with us since, and has had her ups and downs in her health. But she has never shown her will to live without you, in spite of our trying to make her happy and make her life as comfortable as we possibly can. Maybe, this is due to the fact that you both shared an inseparable bond, and she could not come out of the shock.

Like a Hindi song:
DO HANSON KA JODA, BICHAD GAYO RE
GAJAB BHAYO RAMA, JULAM BHAYO RE

I went to give her morning tea and embraced her. She would always ask me my well-being. Today, she uttered something, but I could not follow. She tried again, a couple of times, but no sound. It was then that I realized that she had lost her voice. Called the Doctor, who said to observe for a day and admit her to a hospital tomorrow. Day passed, she ate very little, did not speak, was just smiling looking at us.

7th September 2015

Today morning, when I went to ask Mom for her morning time, I was shocked. Her mouth was open, and her eyes open, but not blinking. Touched her, but she did not move.

Hospitalized. Put on a ventilator. And the ordeal, the trauma, the uncertainty begins. The suffering, Dad, which you went through in the penultimate and final days of your journey, repeats. And I can't see her suffering.

Dad, as you are now united with God, I pray to you to make Mom fine. If this is not possible, please let her come to you, so that you both again become one. I am sorry, being a son, I am asking this, but I am too weak to see her suffering.

I might not have been a good son, leave aside being perfect, but I have not been bad either. I have loved, still love and will always love you and Mom in my lifetime. I might have shown angry outbursts to you and Mom at times, but those were not to hurt you, but with the sole intention of caring and keeping you both in good health. Please pardon me, and don't carry this thought in your minds. My heart and my God know my limitless love for you both.

11th September 2015

Brought Mom home from the hospital today morning, as there was no improvement in her health. Kept a full-time nurse to take care of her. Brought oxygen cylinders, pump to facilitate her breathing.

Just a couple of hours into the morning, Mom breathed her last. My world shattered once again. Shattered completely. Frustration and feelings of helplessness took over me.

My mind kept remembering the words which you used to tell me, Mom, that you will not live beyond 6 months, after Dad. And now, when I think of it, you had left the world on 6th September, when you lost your voice. And it was exactly 6 months. What a bond you both shared, Mom and Dad.

Today, I again pray to the Almighty and to you both. Please let me be your son, in every life of yours and mine. Mom, I wish to be born of your womb, and out of your wedlock with Dad. You were the best parents I could ever have had or imagined.

Mom, you know I have loved you immensely. Limitless, wholeheartedly, with my love as deep as the ocean. Towards the end of your journey, I was short tempered, scolded you sometimes. This stemmed from the realization that I am losing you also, and again, I witness the end, helplessly. Mom, you have always been the silent and sure support of ours, continuously toiling and working. In silence. Never complaining. Never uttering a word.

Pardon me, I seek your pardon with folded hands, with a prayer on my lips, and repentance in my heart.

When You Look Into Your Mother's Eyes, You Know That is the Purest Love You Can Find on This Earth.

– Mitch Albom

4th February 2016

Tomorrow is your birthday, Mom, and we are keeping bhajans at Vadodara. Dads birthday on 12th January was kept in Gurudwara at Mumbai. These 2 dates and 23rd November {your wedding anniversary have been special for me).

The memories I have of both of you, the untold, unspoken love you both had for me, I can never forget in my lifetime., and even in other lives of mine, if they exist. Your thoughts energize me.

R.I.P. departed souls

13th May 2016

Today, I am on a journey to Amravati, sitting alone in 1AC compartment, I am missing you both terribly, Mom and Dad. In the last one year, it has been regular tears for me, remembering you. But; Who cares… who sees? They say: "When you laugh, the world laughs with you…. When you cry, you cry alone." Today I realize the depth of this little line.

Mom, I don't know what happened; but towards the end of your journey, I was a bit harsh to you. For no fault of yours. You were sinking. You knew. We knew. Maybe, this feeling I could not accept. Not so soon, after Dad's demise. I became restless, helpless. Else what justifies my odd behavior towards you, my dearest Mom … who used to love me the most, who cried when I was low, who throughout her life (along with Dad's), always prayed for my happiness and well-being. And whom I loved beyond words which can express. I beg your pardon Mom. I tried to be a good son, and I was successful to a good measure, except towards the end of your journey. Mom and Dad, please don't hold any grudge against me. It was never deliberate in my wildest dreams to trouble or disrespect you… you both know.

Unimaginable.

And the train journey seems endless. Thoughts, memories, instances.

Like, for instance, now, a pair of crows coming to our window, regularly, and waiting till we fed them. Is it a coincidence?

I just remembered, in my school, I had composed a poem (AFTER Munna passed away). Reproducing here, what I can still remember:

Mai jahaan jahaan bhi dekhoon, andhkaar nazar aata hai
Mujhe toh apna jeevan, bekaar nazar aata hai
Yaadon ke silsile mein mai, itna toh kho gaya hoon
Ki mujhko har fiza mein, ujaad nazar aata hai
Dikha na mujhe kabhi, sukh ka ek swapn bhi
Ki mujhko har sukh bekaar nazar aata
Chhupa lo mujhe apne aanchal mein mata
Ki mujhe aapki nazaron mein, pyaar nazar aata hai.

A Father's Goodness is Higher Than the Mountain, a Mother's Goodness is Deeper Than the Sea

– Japanese proverb

3 July 2020

After a hiatus of a few years in picking up bits and pieces of my journey with you, Mom and Dad, I am with you again. I had never left you.... only certain ups and downs in my life.... More downs than ups.... made the hiatus a little longer than I could envisage.

Last 4 years, Samay chakra has moved on, lots of events have taken place.

I have retired from active employment, having reached age 60, and due to health issues, though continue to do consultancy. The start of this year saw the worst pandemic of Coronavirus... lakhs of human lives lost across the world, economies beaten.

In the intermittent years gone by, we have sold your Vadodara home, because my brother was down financially, and was asking for his share-so, it was given to him. Bhabhi also passed away recently, after a bout of ill health. R I P noble soul.

Five years.... and still every day, I have remembered you both, Mom and Dad. Every night, when I pray, I go to your photos.... Seek pardon and seek your blessings.... and invariably, my heart goes heavy.

I can still feel your presence within me, around me. The circles of love of both of you, the protection, the care.... I still yearn. Though I know I will not get it in physical form, but within me, I know.... within my heart, mind and soul that our love still blossoms.

Simplicity was the hallmark of you both. Love was what kept you going…. Love between you as a couple, love for the family, love for humanity. And caring. You were exemplary in everything

After you both left me, my life has seen the lowest ebb. Maybe, within myself, I was lost, I had resigned to fate, I was defeated. I stopped existing. And that was evident in my life. I became short-tempered, irritable… and lonely. Because I had no shoulder to cry on…. no one who would be happy on seeing me…. No one calling me every day…. no hugs and embraces full of warmth and want.

Going back in time, I always think, why you both had so much love for me.? I really could not do much for you in my life. Nothing exceptional or worth a mention. Maybe, the feeling was mutual. Even today, in 2020, there is a total void in my life. I am just existing … but without a reason.

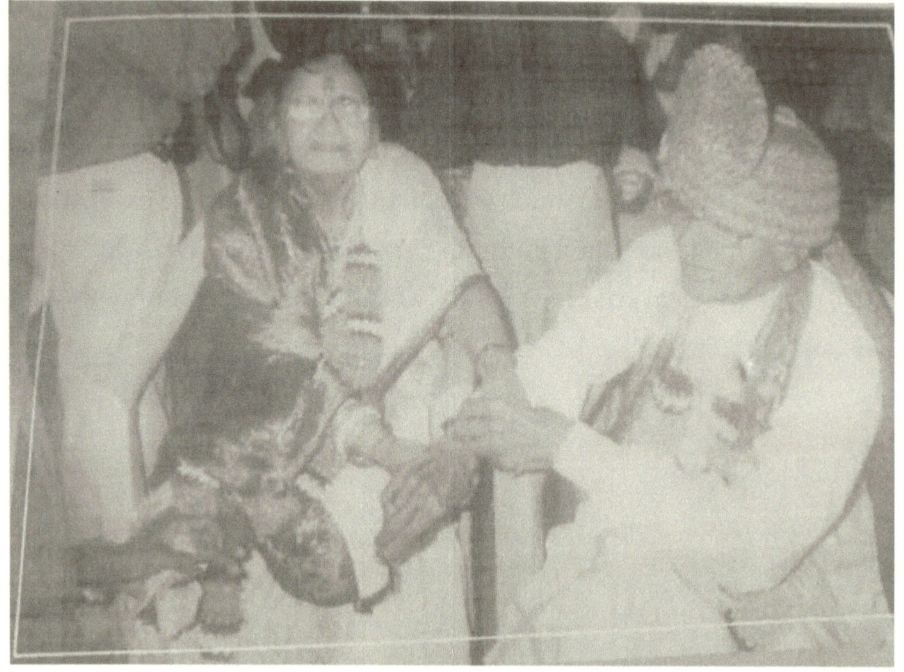

A Mother's Arms and a Father's Guidance Are a Child's Refuge in Life's Storms

– Source unknown

Because all the reasons ended with your departure. My life is superfluous, my smiles superficial.

Sometimes, I suddenly wake up in the middle of the night, when I have a dream. Many a times I have woken up in the morning with a recollection that you were with me the previous night. And even I am surprised that these memories which I had in my dreams I can remember, when I wake up. Do you both also get these feelings? Can you see me? Can you feel me? Can you touch me? Where are you now? I have no inkling.

Mom, you left me in September 2015. And in September 2019, I had a cardiac problem which necessitated angio etc. But due to the renal issues I have, this could not be done. So, took the Ayurveda route. Recovering now.

Another incident happened in September 2019. In the complex where we stay, my wife has many friends – young and also old ladies. One fine evening, when I was returning from work, I saw my wife was sitting with a group of ladies, one of which was quite elderly. I saw her and I was shocked. She resembled you so very much. I sat there for some time. From that day on, whenever I saw her, she smiled and waved at me. And if by chance I did not notice her, she would call out for me. She is a replica of yours, Mom. And nowadays when I meet her, she takes my hand and kisses it lovingly. And she is very fond of my wife too.

10th July 2020

Mom and Dad, Today I request you to please bless my children. Bless them to settle down in their lives – job, marriage etc… Bless them with a long life. Till today, I have seen "WHEN I SEEK …… I RECEIVE".

This has been the untold truth…. whenever I seeked from you, I got, whenever I seeked from GOD, I received. In more ways than one…. If my life has been a mess at times, or if I am down, it is solely my doing. I have only myself to blame. And I accept my shortcomings, my follies.

This brings me to conclude my writing for now. The thoughts will continue till the end of my life. There is an ocean of thoughts within me which wanted to break free, but I believe I have expressed my love and feelings for both of you with my heart. You know me, and you know that each thought of mine, each incident I have narrated…. we have lived all these. And I cherish every moment, every nano-moment that we were together.

Pardon me, Munna
Pardon me, Mom
Pardon me, Dad
Pardon me, God

WHAT YOU BOTH MEANT TO ME

Guiding spirits
Light of my life
Sole basis and reason of my existence
Selfless, exemplary love and caring – pure, eternal, ethereal love

WHAT I MEANT TO YOU BOTH

Reassurance

WHAT I COULD ACHIEVE

With a limited measure of success, I tried to make your lives comfortable and happy, as a son would want and wish.

Our love was reciprocated and you both and me, understood it, felt it, experienced it.

WHAT I COULD NOT ACHIEVE

Though I wanted to, I could not give you total support and caring.

This thought and my shortcomings, I shall always remember and regret my inabilities, all through my life... till my last breath.

Pardon me, my MAKERS... MY GOD AND GODDESS in human form.

No Matter How Far We Come, Our Parents Are Always in Us

– Brad Meltzer

www.ingramcontent.com/pod-product-compliance
Lightning Source LLC
LaVergne TN
LVHW091235150826
845673LV00003B/1155

* 9 7 9 8 8 9 1 3 3 4 3 5 9 *